crocheted HATS for the beginner

You know you look marvelous in a hat—

and these fabulous fashions are so easy to crochet, you'll want to make them all. There's a fetching red tam, a glamorous peacock rolled-brim, a plush brown riding cap—a total of six styles by Mary Estok Nolfi that will flatter your face. Come to think of it, aren't your friends going to want some of these tempting toppers, too? Treat them to a black-and-white hat with a perky blossom and an adjustable brim. Or how about a simple blue-and-grey number with a sporty rolled edge? There's even a dressy black design that makes every occasion a little more elegant. Choose your favorite pattern and get started, because an entire wardrobe of original hats is at your fingertips.

MEET MARY ESTOK NOLFI

Like many of today's crochet designers, Mary Estok Nolfi learned to crochet when she was very young. But Mary's initiation into the craft at age seven did not occur under the guidance of her mother or grandmother. Mary learned by following the instructions in a kit to make a small stuffed toy poodle. Once the little poodle was completed, Mary was hooked. She's been designing and teaching crochet, as well as other needle arts, ever since.

Mary holds a degree in Marketing which she followed with intense post-graduate studies in Architectural Design. She also pursues Interdisciplinary Studies in Fine Crafts whenever time allows.

"I started my own business back in 1973," says Mary. "M.E. and Co. has been my business moniker through all of my art and mixed media endeavors

since then. But I've always come back to the needle arts. Especially crochet, embroidery, and hand sewing. The needle arts seem to provide me with a sense of peace and comfort. Somehow, I feel 'at home' with my hooks and needles."

Mary is intent upon sharing that feeling of peace and comfort in her crochet designs. I'd like to believe that crochet is a sort of therapy for anything else," she explains. "That's why I have designed my latest business venture, a website dedicated to crochet, as a sanctuary for all of us crochet addicts—or crochet addicts-to-be."

Visit Mary at www.crochetasylum.com. "You'll find crochet therapy of all kinds while you're visiting." Mary says. "I'm the head inmate, and you are always welcome!"

Leisure Arts, Inc.
Little Rock, Arkansas

WELCOME TO THE WORLD OF CROCHETED HATS!

Whether you have crocheted for years or have just now mastered the basic stitches, you can make these hats.

Our six stylish hats are made with the most basic crochet stitches. All the patterns are rated EASY and are arranged from the most simple to the most difficult.

The hats are all crocheted in the round and each pattern lists what stitches are used. Our first three hat patterns use only the simplest of stitches—chain, slip stitch, single crochet, half double crochet, and double crochet.

Our General Instructions section provides you with step-by-step basic stitch instructions on pages 6 and 7 if you are out of practice or just need a refresher.

There are so many great yarns in the stores now. Chenille and suede work up quickly and are absolutely luscious to touch while bouclés and ribbons add texture. Wools are still a winter staple. And, cottons will keep you cool on those long, lazy summer outings.

So, chose yarns that will make you feel good and look great on you. And, pick up a crochet hook and have fun making our head-turning, eye-catching hats.

GENERAL INSTRUCTIONS

ABBREVIATIONS

ch(s)	chain(s)
cm	centimeters
dc	double crochet(s)
hdc	half double crochet(s)
mm	millimeters
Rnd(s)	Round(s)
sc	single crochet(s)
sp(s)	space(s)
st(s)	stitch(es)
tr	treble crochet(s)
YO	yarn over

★ — work instructions following ★ as many **more** times as indicated in addition to the first time.

( ) or [ ] — work enclosed instructions **as many** times as specified by the number immediately following **or** contains explanatory remarks.

colon (:) — the number(s) given after a colon at the end of a row or round denote(s) the number of stitches or spaces you should have on that row or round.

CROCHET TERMINOLOGY	
UNITED STATES	**INTERNATIONAL**
slip stitch (slip st) =	single crochet (sc)
single crochet (sc) =	double crochet (dc)
half double crochet (hdc) =	half treble crochet (htr)
double crochet (dc) =	treble crochet (tr)
treble crochet (tr) =	double treble crochet (dtr)
double treble crochet (dtr) =	triple treble crochet (ttr)
triple treble crochet (tr tr) =	quadruple treble crochet (qtr)
skip =	miss

GAUGE

To make sure your hat comes out fitting just right, it is very essential that you match the GAUGE that is given with each hat's instructions. BEFORE beginning your hat, make the sample SWATCH, working the same number of rounds given with the gauge swatch's instructions. Some of the swatches have more than one strand of yarn used at the same time. Use yarns that are the same weights shown by the small yarn ball symbols with a number in them. The Yarn chart on page 4 explains more about these yarn icons and the yarn weights they signify. Be sure you use the crochet hook we give in the instructions, as well.

After making your SWATCH, measure it. Your GAUGE is correct if you get the same measurements and have the same number of rounds as the sample swatch. If your swatch does not measure the same as ours, recheck the number of rounds to make sure you have made the same number as the instructions.

If the rounds are correct but your swatch is BIGGER than specified, remake your swatch with a SMALLER hook.

If the rounds are correct but your swatch is SMALLER than specified, remake your swatch with a LARGER hook.

You may have to try more than once to find the right size hook.

Keep working your swatch, changing your hook size until you get the same gauge as in the pattern; then use that hook to make your hat.

CROCHET HOOKS													
U.S.	B-1	C-2	D-3	E-4	F-5	G-6	H-8	I-9	J-10	K-10½	N	P	Q
Metric - mm	2.25	2.75	3.25	3.5	3.75	4	5	5.5	6	6.5	9	10	15

Yarn Weight Symbol & Names	SUPER FINE 1	FINE 2	LIGHT 3	MEDIUM 4	BULKY 5	SUPER BULKY 6
Type of Yarns in Category	Sock, Fingering Baby	Sport, Baby	DK, Light Worsted	Worsted, Afghan, Aran	Chunky, Craft, Rug	Bulky, Roving
Crochet Gauge Ranges in Single Crochet to 4" (10 cm)	21-32 sts	16-20 sts	12-17 sts	11-14 sts	8-11 sts	5-9 sts
Advised Hook Size Range	B-1 to E-4	E-4 to 7	7 to I-9	I-9 to K-10.5	K-10.5 to M-13	M-13 and larger

●□□□ BEGINNER	Projects for first-time crocheters using basic stitches. Minimal shaping.
●■□□ EASY	Projects using yarn with basic stitches, repetitive stitch patterns, simple color changes, and simple shaping and finishing.
●■■□ INTERMEDIATE	Projects using a variety of techniques, such as basic lace patterns or color patterns, mid-level shaping and finishing.
●■■■ EXPERIENCED	Projects with intricate stitch patterns, techniques and dimension, such as non-repeating patterns, multi-color techniques, fine threads, small hooks, detailed shaping and refined finishing.

HINTS

As in all crocheted pieces, good finishing techniques make a big difference in the quality of the piece. Make a habit of taking care of loose ends as you work. Thread a yarn needle with the yarn end. With **wrong** side facing, weave the needle through several stitches, then reverse the direction and weave it back through several stitches. When the ends are secure, clip them off close to the work.

JOINING WITH SC

When instructed to join with sc, begin with a slip knot on hook. Insert hook in stitch or space indicated, YO and pull up a loop **(Fig. 1a)**, YO and draw through both loops on hook **(Fig. 1b)**.

Fig. 1a

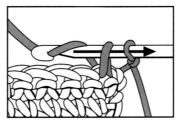

Fig. 1b

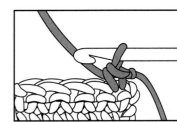

BACK OR FRONT LOOP ONLY

Work only in loop(s) indicated by arrow (Fig. 2).

Fig. 2

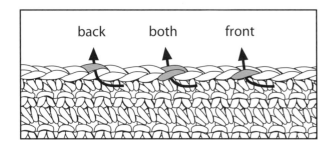

FREE LOOPS

After working in Back or Front Loops Only on a row or round, there will be a ridge of unused loops called the free loops. Later, when instructed to work in the free loops of the same row or round, work in these loops (Fig. 3).

Fig. 3

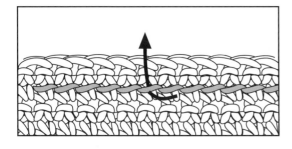

REVERSE SINGLE CROCHET

Working from **left** to **right**, ★ insert hook in st to right of hook (Fig. 4a), YO and draw through, under and to left of loop on hook (2 loops on hook) (Fig. 4b), YO and draw through both loops on hook (Fig. 4c) (reverse sc made, Fig. 4d); repeat from ★ around.

Fig. 4a

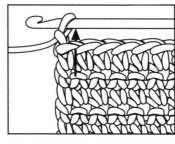

Fig. 4b

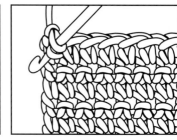

Fig. 4c

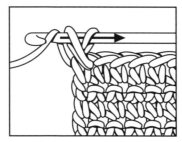

Fig. 4d

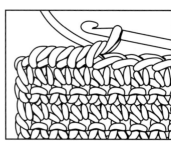

BASIC CROCHET STITCHES

CHAIN (abbreviated ch)

To work a chain stitch, begin with a slip knot on the hook. Bring the yarn **over** hook from back to front, catching the yarn with the hook and turning the hook slightly toward you to keep the yarn from slipping off. Draw the yarn through the slip knot **(Fig. 5)**.

Fig.5

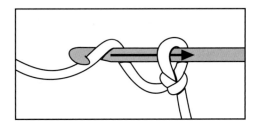

WORKING INTO THE CHAIN

Method 1: Insert hook into back ridge of each chain **(Fig. 6a)**.
Method 2: Insert hook under top two strands of each chain **(Fig. 6b)**.

Fig. 6a

Fig. 6b

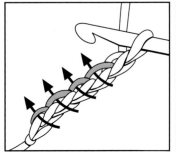 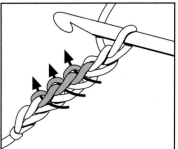

SLIP STITCH (abbreviated slip st)

To work a slip stitch, insert hook in stitch indicated, YO and draw through st and through loop on hook **(Fig. 7)**.

Fig. 7

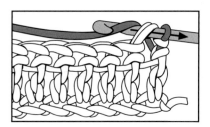

SINGLE CROCHET (abbreviated sc)

Insert hook in stitch indicated, YO and pull up a loop, YO and draw through both loops on hook **(Fig. 8)**.

Fig. 8

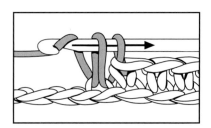

HALF DOUBLE CROCHET
(abbreviated hdc)
YO, insert hook in stitch indicated, YO and pull up a loop, YO and draw through all 3 loops on hook *(Fig. 9)*.

Fig. 9

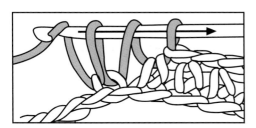

DOUBLE CROCHET *(abbreviated dc)*
YO, insert hook in stitch indicated, YO and pull up a loop (3 loops on hook), YO and draw through 2 loops on hook *(Fig. 10a)*, YO and draw through remaining 2 loops on hook *(Fig. 10b)*.

Fig. 10a   **Fig. 10b**

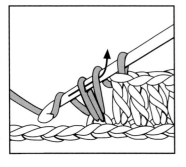 

TREBLE CROCHET *(abbreviated tr)*
YO twice, insert hook in stitch indicated, YO and pull up a loop (4 loops on hook) *(Fig. 11a)*, (YO and draw through 2 loops on hook) 3 times *(Fig. 11b)*.

Fig. 11a

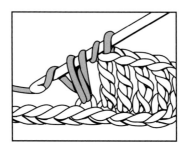

Fig. 11b

1. SOPHISTICATED LADY

Shown on page 12.

■■□□ EASY

Stitches used: Chain, slip stitch, single crochet, half double crochet, double crochet

Finished Size: Adult
Head Circumference: 21½" (54.5 cm)

MATERIALS

SUPER BULKY **6**

Super Bulky Weight Chenille Yarn
[100 yards (91.4 meters) per skein]:
2 skeins

MEDIUM **4**

100% Cotton Medium Weight Yarn
[5 ounces, 236 yards
(140 grams, 215 meters) per ball]:
1 ball
Crochet hook, size J (6 mm) **or** size needed for gauge

GAUGE SWATCH: 3³/₄" (9.5 cm) diameter
Work same as Crown through Rnd 2.

CROWN

Holding one strand of **each** yarn together, ch 5; join with slip st to form a ring.

Rnd 1 (Right side)**:** Ch 3 **(counts as first dc, now and throughout)**, 11 dc in ring; join with slip st to first dc: 12 dc.

Note: Loop a short piece of yarn around any stitch to mark Rnd 1 as **right** side.

Rnd 2: Ch 3, dc in same st, 2 dc in next dc and in each dc around; join with slip st to first dc: 24 dc.

Rnd 3: Ch 3, 2 dc in next dc, (dc in next dc, 2 dc in next dc) around; join with slip st to first dc: 36 dc.

Rnd 4: Ch 3, dc in next dc, 2 dc in next dc, (dc in next 2 dc, 2 dc in next dc) around; join with slip st to first dc: 48 dc.

Rnds 5-8: Ch 3, dc in next dc and in each dc around; join with slip st to first dc.

Rnd 9: Ch 2, hdc in same st and in each dc around; skip beginning ch-2 and join with slip st to first hdc, do **not** finish off.

BRIM

Rnd 1: Ch 1, sc in same st and in next 2 hdc, 2 sc in next hdc, (sc in next 3 hdc, 2 sc in next hdc) around; join with slip st to first sc: 60 sc.

Rnd 2: Ch 1, sc in same st and in next 3 sc, 2 sc in next sc, (sc in next 4 sc, 2 sc in next sc) around; join with slip st to first sc: 72 sc.

Rnd 3: Ch 1, sc in same st and in each sc around; join with slip st to first sc.

Rnd 4: Ch 1, sc in same st and in next 4 sc, 2 sc in next sc, (sc in next 5 sc, 2 sc in next sc) around; join with slip st to first sc: 84 sc.

Rnd 5: Ch 1, sc in same st and in each sc around; join with slip st to first sc.

Rnd 6: Ch 1, sc in same st and in next 5 sc, 2 sc in next sc, (sc in next 7 sc, 2 sc in next sc) around; join with slip st to first sc: 96 sc.

Rnd 7: Ch 1, sc in same st and in each sc around; join with slip st to first sc.

Rnd 8: Ch 2, hdc in same st and in each sc around; skip beginning ch-2 and join with slip st to first hdc.

Rnd 9: Ch 1, **turn**; slip st in first hdc and in each hdc around; join with slip st to first slip st, finish off.

TIP: This slip stitch edge is a simple finishing technique that gives the Brim a more stable quality and finished look.

2. GLAMOROUS LADY

Shown on page 13.

◼◼◻◻ EASY

Stitches used: Chain, slip stitch, single crochet, half double crochet, double crochet

Finished Size: Adult
Head Circumference: 21½" (54.5 cm)

MATERIALS
Super Bulky Weight Chenille Yarn 🟡6
   [100 yards (91.4 meters) per skein]:
      2 skeins
100% Cotton Medium Weight Yarn 🟡4
   [5 ounces, 236 yards
      (140 grams, 215 meters) per ball]:
      1 ball
Crochet hook, size J (6 mm) **or** size needed for gauge

GAUGE SWATCH: 2¾" (7 cm) diameter
Work same as Crown through Rnd 2.

CROWN
Holding one strand of **each** yarn together, ch 5; join with slip st to form a ring.

Rnd 1 (Right side)**:** Ch 3 **(counts as first dc, now and throughout)**, 11 dc in ring; join with slip st to first dc: 12 dc.

Note: Loop a short piece of yarn around any stitch to mark Rnd 1 as **right** side.

Rnd 2: Ch 1, 2 sc in same st and in each dc around; join with slip st to first sc: 24 sc.

Rnd 3: Ch 1, sc in same st and in each st around; join with slip st to first sc.

Rnd 4: Ch 3, 2 dc in next sc, (dc in next sc, 2 dc in next sc) around; join with slip st to first dc: 36 dc.

Rnd 5: Ch 2, hdc in same st and in next 2 dc, 2 hdc in next dc, (hdc in next 2 dc, 2 hdc in next dc) around; skip beginning ch-2 and join with slip st to first hdc: 48 hdc.

Rnd 6: Repeat Rnd 3.

Rnds 7-11: Ch 2, hdc in same st and in each st around; skip beginning ch-2 and join with slip st to first hdc, do **not** finish off.

BRIM
Rnd 1: Ch 2, hdc in same st and in next 2 hdc, 2 hdc in next hdc, (hdc in next 3 hdc, 2 hdc in next hdc) around; skip beginning ch-2 and join with slip st to first hdc: 60 hdc.

Rnd 2: Ch 1, sc in same st and in each st around; join with slip st to first sc.

Rnd 3: Ch 2, hdc in same st and in next 3 sc, 2 hdc in next sc, (hdc in next 4 sc, 2 hdc in next sc) around; skip beginning ch-2 and join with slip st to first hdc: 72 hdc.

Rnd 4: Repeat Rnd 2.

Rnd 5: Ch 1, sc in same st and in next 4 sc, 2 sc in next sc, (sc in next 5 sc, 2 sc in next sc) around; join with slip st to first sc: 84 sc.

Rnds 6 and 7: Repeat Rnd 2 twice.

Rnd 8: Ch 1, sc in same st and in next 5 sc, 2 sc in next sc, (sc in next 6 sc, 2 sc in next sc) around; join with slip st to first sc: 96 sc.

Rnd 9: Repeat Rnd 2.

Rnd 10: Ch 1, **turn**; slip st in first sc and in each sc around; join with slip st to first slip st, finish off.

TIP: This slip stitch edge is a simple finishing technique that gives the Brim a more stable quality and finished look.

3. LADY IN RED _____

Shown on page 16.

▬▬☐☐ EASY

Stitches used: Chain, slip stitch, single crochet, half double crochet, double crochet
Techniques used: decrease, joining new yarn

Finished Size: Adult
Head Circumference: 21½" (54.5 cm)

MATERIALS
 Super Bulky Weight Bouclé Yarn ⬛ SUPER BULKY 6
 [6 ounces, 148 yards
  (170 grams, 135 meters) per skein]:
  1 skein
 Super Bulky Weight Chenille Yarn
 [100 yards (91 meters) per skein]:
  1 skein
 Crochet hooks, sizes J (6 mm) **and** K (6.5 mm)
  or sizes needed for gauge
 Yarn needle
 Sewing needle and thread
 ⁷⁄₈" (22 mm) Button - 1

GAUGE SWATCH: 2¾" (7 cm) diameter
Work same as Crown through Rnd 3.

STITCH GUIDE

DECREASE (uses next 2 dc)
★ YO, insert hook in **next** dc, YO and pull up a loop, YO and draw through 2 loops on hook; repeat from ★ once **more**, YO and draw through all 3 loops on hook **(counts as one dc)**.

CROWN

With larger size hook and Bouclé yarn, ch 4; join with slip st to form a ring.

Rnd 1 (Right side)**:** Ch 1, 10 sc in ring; join with slip st to first sc.

Note: Loop a short piece of yarn around any stitch to mark Rnd 1 as **right** side.

Rnd 2: Ch 1, 2 sc in same st and in each sc around; join with slip st to first sc: 20 sc.

Rnd 3: Ch 1, sc in same st and in each sc around; join with slip st to first sc.

Rnd 4: Ch 3 **(counts as first dc, now and throughout)**, 2 dc in next sc, (dc in next sc, 2 dc in next sc) around; join with slip st to first dc: 30 dc.

Rnd 5: Ch 3, dc in next dc, 2 dc in next dc, (dc in next 2 dc, 2 dc in next dc) around; join with slip st to first dc: 40 dc.

Rnd 6: Ch 3, dc in next 2 dc, 2 dc in next dc, (dc in next 3 dc, 2 dc in next dc) around; join with slip st to first dc: 50 dc.

Rnds 7 and 8: Ch 3, dc in next 3 dc, 2 dc in next dc, (dc in next 4 dc, 2 dc in next dc) around; join with slip st to first dc: 72 dc.

Rnds 9 and 10: Ch 3, dc in next dc and in each dc around; join with slip st to first dc.

Rnd 11: Ch 3, dc in next 3 dc, decrease, (dc in next 4 dc, decrease) around; join with slip st to first dc: 60 dc.

Rnd 12: Ch 3, dc in next 2 dc, decrease, (dc in next 3 dc, decrease) around; join with slip st to first dc, finish off: 48 dc.

BAND

Rnd 1: With **right** side facing and using smaller size hook, join Chenille yarn with slip st in same st as joining; ch 2, hdc in same st and in each dc around; skip beginning ch-2 and join with slip st to first hdc.

Rnds 2 and 3: Ch 1, sc in same st and in each st around; join with slip st to first sc.

Trim: Rotate Hat so that the Crown is away from you, with **right** side facing and keeping yarn to **wrong** side, slip st in next 2 sc rnds and in hdc rnd; working in same dc as Rnd 1 of Band, slip st in each dc around; join with slip st to first slip st on dc rnd, finish off.

FLOWER

Stitches used: Chain, slip stitch, single crochet, half double crochet

With Chenille yarn and larger size hook, ch 4; join with slip st to form a ring.

Rnd 1 (Right side)**:** Ch 1, 10 sc in ring; join with slip st to first sc.

Note: Loop a short piece of yarn around any stitch to mark Rnd 1 as **right** side.

Rnd 2: Ch 4, skip next sc, ★ slip st in next sc, ch 4, skip next sc; repeat from ★ around; join with slip st to joining slip st: 5 ch-4 sps.

Rnd 3: ★ Ch 2, 4 hdc in next ch-4 sp, slip st in next slip st; repeat from ★ around; finish off leaving long end for sewing: 5 petals.

With sewing needle and thread, sew button to center of Flower. Thread yarn needle with long end and sew Flower to Band over joinings.

1

2

4. MY FAIR LADY

Shown on page 17.

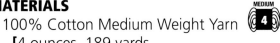 EASY

Stitches used: Chain, slip stitch, single crochet, half double crochet, double crochet, treble crochet

Finished Size: Adult
Head Circumference: 21½" (54.5 cm)

MATERIALS
100% Cotton Medium Weight Yarn **MEDIUM 4**
  [4 ounces, 189 yards
    (113 grams, 172 meters) per ball]:
    Variegated - 1 ball
  [5 ounces, 236 yards
    (140 grams, 215 meters) per ball]:
    White - 1 ball
    Black - 1 ball
Bulky Weight Ladder Ribbon Yarn **BULKY 5**
  [1¾ ounces, 115 yards
    (50 grams, 105 meters) per ball]:
    2 balls
Crochet hooks, sizes F (3.75 mm), G (4 mm),
  and H (5 mm) **or** sizes needed for gauge
2½" (6.5 cm) piece of Black felt for Flower
1" (2.5 cm) Pin back
Sewing needle and thread
Yarn needle

GAUGE SWATCH: 2¾" (7 cm) diameter
Work same as Crown through Rnd 2.

STITCH GUIDE

TREBLE CROCHET *(abbreviated tr)*
YO twice, insert hook in st indicated, YO and pull up a loop (4 loops on hook), (YO and draw through 2 loops on hook) 3 times.

CROWN
Holding one strand of Cotton Variegated and Ribbon yarn together and using largest size hook, ch 4; join with slip st to form a ring.

Rnd 1 (Right side): Ch 3 **(counts as first dc, now and throughout)**, 11 dc in ring; join with slip st to first dc: 12 dc.

Note: Loop a short piece of yarn around any stitch to mark Rnd 1 as **right** side.

Rnd 2: Ch 3, dc in same st, 2 dc in next dc and in each dc around; join with slip st to first dc: 24 dc.

Rnd 3: Ch 3, 2 dc in next dc, (dc in next dc, 2 dc in next dc) around; join with slip st to first dc: 36 dc.

Rnd 4: Ch 3, dc in next dc, 2 dc in next dc, (dc in next 2 dc, 2 dc in next dc) around; join with slip st to first dc: 48 dc.

Rnd 5: Ch 3, dc in next 2 dc, 2 dc in next dc, (dc in next 3 dc, 2 dc in next dc) around; join with slip st to first dc: 60 dc.

Rnd 6: Ch 3, dc in next 3 dc, 2 dc in next dc, (dc in next 4 dc, 2 dc in next dc) around; join with slip st to first dc: 72 dc.

Rnd 7: Ch 1, sc in same st and in each st around; join with slip st to first sc.

Rnd 8: Ch 2, hdc in same st and in each sc around; skip beginning ch-2 and join with slip st to first hdc.

Rnds 9-16: Repeat Rnds 7 and 8, 4 times; do **not** finish off.

BRIM
Change to medium size hook.

Rnd 1: Ch 1, sc in same st and in next 4 hdc, 2 sc in next hdc, (sc in next 5 hdc, 2 sc in next hdc) around; join with slip st to first sc: 84 sc.

Rnd 2: Ch 1, sc in same st and in each sc around; join with slip st to first sc.

Rnd 3: Ch 1, sc in same st and in next 5 sc, 2 sc in next sc, (sc in next 6 sc, 2 sc in next sc) around; join with slip st to first sc: 96 sc.

Rnd 4: Ch 1, sc in same st and in each sc around; join with slip st to first sc.

Rnd 5: Ch 1, sc in same st and in next 6 sc, 2 sc in next sc, (sc in next 7 sc, 2 sc in next sc) around; join with slip st to first sc: 108 sc.

Rnd 6: Ch 1, sc in same st and in each sc around; join with slip st to first sc.

Rnd 7: Ch 1, sc in same st and in next 7 sc, 2 sc in next sc, (sc in next 8 sc, 2 sc in next sc) around; join with slip st to first sc: 120 sc.

Rnds 8 and 9: Ch 1, sc in same st and in each sc around; join with slip st to first sc.

Rnd 10: Ch 1, sc in same st and in next 8 sc, 2 sc in next sc, (sc in next 9 sc, 2 sc in next sc) around; join with slip st to first sc: 132 sc.

Rnd 11: Ch 1, sc in same st and in each sc around; join with slip st to first sc.

Rnd 12: Ch 1, **turn**; slip st in first sc and in each sc around; join with slip st to first slip st, finish off.

TIP: The Brim on this Hat will be very pliable. Therefore, you will be able to adjust the Brim by turning it up or down or half and half. It's your choice.

FLOWER

Stitches used: Chain, slip stitch, single crochet, half double crochet, double crochet, treble crochet
Technique used: joining new yarn with single crochet

With one strand of Cotton Variegated yarn and using smallest size hook, ch 50.

Row 1 (Right side)**:** Sc in second ch from hook and in each ch across: 49 sc.

Note: Loop a short piece of yarn around any stitch to mark Row 1 as **right** side.

Row 2: Ch 2 **(counts as first hdc)**, turn; hdc in next sc and in each sc across; finish off.

Row 3: With **right** side facing, join White with sc in first hdc **(Figs. 1a & b, page 4)**; ★ hdc in next hdc, dc in next hdc, 3 tr in next hdc, dc in next hdc, hdc in next hdc, sc in next hdc; repeat from ★ across: 65 sts.

Row 4: Turn; slip st in first sc, ★ sc in next hdc, (2 sc in next st, sc in next st) 3 times, slip in next sc; repeat from ★ across; finish off leaving a long end for sewing: 89 sts.

Row 5: With **right** side facing, join Black with sc in first slip st; (ch 3, skip next st, sc in next st) across, slip st in end of each row across to beginning ch.

Stamen: ★ Ch 12, slip st in sixth ch from hook and in last 6 chs; repeat from ★ 2 times **more**; finish off leaving a long end for sewing.

FINISHING

Thread yarn needle with long end of Black. Roll piece having Stamen to center **right** side; then tack in place.

Thread yarn needle with long end of White. Tuck and ruffle petals in a circular fashion, tacking each ruffle in place and keeping all yarn ends to the back of the Flower; secure end.

Cut a 1³/₄" (4.5 cm) diameter circle from felt and sew to center back of the Flower. With sewing needle and thread, sew a pin back to center back working through both felt and Flower to make the pin secure.

TIP: The Flower can be worn on the Hat or as a clothing accessory.

3

4

5. LADY SINGS THE BLUES

Shown on page 20.

∎∎☐☐ **EASY**

Stitches used: Chain, slip stitch, single crochet, half double crochet, double crochet, reverse single crochet

Technique used: Working in Back Loop Only

Finished Size: Adult
Head Circumference: 21½" (54.5 cm)

MATERIALS

Bulky Weight Bouclé Yarn **BULKY 5**
[6 ounces, 185 yards
(170 grams, 169 meters) per skein]:
1 skein
Bulky Weight Mohair Novelty Yarn
[1¾ ounces, 82 yards
(50 grams, 75 meters) per ball]:
2 balls
Crochet hooks, sizes H (5 mm) **and** I (5.5 mm)
or sizes needed for gauge

GAUGE SWATCH: 3¼" (8.25 cm) diameter
Work same as Crown through Rnd 2.

CROWN

Holding one strand of **each** yarn together and using larger size hook, ch 4; join with slip st to form a ring.

Rnd 1 (Right side): Ch 3 **(counts as first dc, now and throughout)**, 11 dc in ring; join with slip st to first dc: 12 dc.

Note: Loop a short piece of yarn around any stitch to mark Rnd 1 as **right** side.

Rnd 2: Ch 3, dc in same st, 2 dc in next dc and in each dc around; join with slip st to first dc: 24 dc.

Rnd 3: Ch 3, 2 dc in next dc, (dc in next dc, 2 dc in next dc) around; join with slip st to first dc: 36 dc.

Rnd 4: Ch 3, dc in next dc, 2 dc in next dc, (dc in next 2 dc, 2 dc in next dc) around; join with slip st to first dc: 48 dc.

Rnd 5: Ch 3, dc in next 6 dc, 2 dc in next dc, (dc in next 7 dc, 2 dc in next dc) around; join with slip st to first dc: 54 dc.

Rnds 6-10: Ch 3, dc in next dc and in each dc around; join with slip st to first dc.

Rnd 11: Ch 2, hdc in same st and in next 7 dc, 2 hdc in next dc, (hdc in next 8 dc, 2 hdc in next dc) around; skip beginning ch-2 and join with slip st to first hdc, do **not** finish off: 60 hdc.

BRIM

Change to smaller size hook.

Rnd 1: Ch 3, working in Back Loops Only **(Fig. 2, page 5)**, dc in next 3 hdc, 2 dc in next hdc, (dc in next 4 hdc, 2 dc in next hdc) around; join with slip st to first dc: 72 dc.

Rnd 2: Ch 3, working in both loops, dc in next 4 dc, 2 dc in next dc, (dc in next 5 dc, 2 dc in next dc) around; join with slip st to first dc: 84 dc.

Rnd 3: Ch 3, dc in next 5 dc, 2 dc in next dc, (dc in next 6 dc, 2 dc in next dc) around; join with slip st to first dc: 96 dc.

Rnd 4: Ch 2, hdc in same st and in each dc around; skip beginning ch-2 and join with slip st to first hdc.

Rnd 5: Ch 1, working from **left** to **right**, work reverse sc in same st and in each hdc around *(Figs. 4a-d, page 5)*; join with slip st to first st, finish off.

TIP: The reverse sc makes a wonderful finishing technique for a rolled edge.

HATBAND

Holding one strand of **each** yarn together and using larger size hook, ch 106, slip st in second ch from hook and in each ch across; finish off.
Tie a knot close to each end. Wrap Hatband around the base of Crown; then tie a square knot to hold Hatband loosely in place.

6. SPORTY LADY

Shown on page 21.

◖■■◻◻◗ **EASY**

Stitches used: Chain, slip stitch, single crochet, half double crochet, double crochet
Techniques used: Working in Front Loop Only, working in free loops, crocheting two pieces together

Finished Size: Adult
Head Circumference: 21½" (54.5 cm)

MATERIALS

Bulky Weight Suede Yarn **BULKY 5**
[3 ounces, 122 yards
(85 grams, 110 meters) per skein]:
1 skein
Crochet hook, size G (4 mm) **or** size needed for gauge

GAUGE SWATCH: 3" (7.5 cm) diameter
Work same as Crown through Rnd 2.

CROWN

Ch 4; join with slip st to form a ring.

Rnd 1 (Right side)**:** Ch 3 **(counts as first dc, now and throughout)**, 11 dc in ring; join with slip st to first dc: 12 dc.

Note: Loop a short piece of yarn around any stitch to mark Rnd 1 as **right** side.

Rnd 2: Ch 3, dc in same st, 2 dc in next dc and in each dc around; join with slip st to first dc: 24 dc.

Rnd 3: Ch 3, 2 dc in next dc, (dc in next dc, 2 dc in next dc) around; join with slip st to first dc: 36 dc.

Rnd 4: Ch 3, dc in next dc, 2 dc in next dc, (dc in next 2 dc, 2 dc in next dc) around; join with slip st to first dc: 48 dc.

Instructions continued on page 22.

5

6

Rnd 5: Ch 3, dc in next 2 dc, 2 dc in next dc, (dc in next 3 dc, 2 dc in next dc) around; join with slip st to first dc: 60 dc.

Rnds 6-9: Ch 3, dc in next dc and in each dc around; join with slip st to first dc.

Rnd 10: Ch 1, sc in same st and in each dc around; join with slip st to Front Loop Only of first sc *(Fig. 2, page 5)*, do **not** finish off.

BILL
TOP
Row 1: Ch 1, working in Front Loops Only, sc in next 5 sc, hdc in next 5 sc, dc in next sc, 2 dc in next sc, dc in next 4 sc, 2 dc in next sc, dc in next sc, hdc in next 5 sc, sc in next 5 sc, slip st in next sc, leave remaining 30 sc unworked: 32 sts.

Row 2: Ch 1, turn; skip first slip st, slip st in next sc, sc in next 4 sc, hdc in next 2 hdc, 2 hdc in next hdc, hdc in next 2 hdc, dc in next 10 dc, hdc in next 2 hdc, 2 hdc in next hdc, hdc in next 2 hdc, sc in next 4 sc, skip next sc, slip st in joining slip st.

Row 3: Ch 1, turn; skip first slip st, slip st in next sc, sc in next 3 sc, hdc in next 7 sts, 2 dc in next dc, dc in next 2 dc, 2 dc in each of next 2 dc, dc in next 2 dc, 2 dc in next dc, hdc in next 7 sts, sc in next 3 sc, skip next sc, slip st in last slip st: 34 sts.

Row 4: Ch 1, turn; skip first slip st, slip st in next sc, sc in next 2 sc, hdc in next 3 hdc, 2 hdc in next hdc, hdc in next 5 sts, dc in next 2 dc, (2 dc in next dc, dc in next 2 dc) twice, hdc in next 5 sts, 2 hdc in next hdc, hdc in next 3 hdc, sc in next 2 sc, skip next sc, slip st in last slip st: 36 sts.

Row 5: Ch 1, turn; skip first slip st, slip st in next 2 sc, sc in next 3 hdc, hdc in next 2 hdc, 2 hdc in next hdc, hdc in next 2 hdc, dc in next 7 sts, 2 dc in next dc, dc in next 7 sts, hdc in next 2 hdc, 2 hdc in next hdc, hdc in next 2 hdc, sc in next 3 sts, skip next sc, slip st in end of each row across to Row 1; do **not** finish off.

BOTTOM
Row 1: Ch 1, turn; working in free loops of sc on Rnd 10 of Crown and in front of Top *(Fig. 3, page 5)*; sc in next 5 sc, hdc in next 5 sc, dc in next sc, 2 dc in next sc, dc in next 4 sc, 2 dc in next sc, dc in next sc, hdc in next 5 sc, sc in next 5 sc, slip st in next sc, leave remaining 30 sc unworked: 32 sts.

Rows 2-5: Work same as Top.

JOINING AND EDGING
Ch 1, turn; working through **both** thicknesses on Top and Bottom, sc in end of each row and in each st across Bill, slip st in next sc and in each sc on Rnd 10 of Crown; join with slip st to first sc, finish off.

Tip: The double thickness gives the Bill stability.

YARN INFORMATION

Each hat in this leaflet was made with Super Bulky, Bulky, and/or Medium Weight Yarn. Any brand of yarn in the specified weight may be used. It is best to refer to the yardage/meters when determining how many balls or skeins to purchase. Remember, to arrive at the finished size, it is the GAUGE/TENSION that is important, not the brand of yarn.

For your convenience, listed below are the specific yarns used to create our photography models.

1. SOPHISTICATED LADY
Lion Brand® Chenille Thick & Quick®
#153 Black
Lion Brand® Lion Cotton
#153 Black

2. GLAMOROUS LADY
Lion Brand® Chenille Thick & Quick®
#122 Peacock
Lion Brand® Lion Cotton
#131 Fern Green

3. LADY IN RED
Red Heart® Light & Lofty
#9376 Wine
Lion Brand® Chenille Thick & Quick
#189 Wine

4. MY FAIR LADY
Lion Brand® Lion Cotton
Variegated - #201 Salt and Pepper
White - #100 White
Black - #153 Black
Lion Brand® Trellis
Ribbon - #301 Night Life

5. LADY SINGS THE BLUES
Lion Brand® Homespun®
#321 Williamsburg
Lion Brand® Moonlight Mohair
#205 Glacier Bay

6. SPORTY LADY
Lion Brand® Lion Suede
#126 Coffee

Production Team:
Instructional Editor - Lois J. Long
Technical Editor - Cathy Hardy
Editorial Writer - Susan McManus Johnson
Artist - Elaine Wheat
Senior Artist - Lora Puls
Photo Stylist - Angela Alexander
Photographer - Jason Masters

We have made every effort to ensure that these instructions are accurate and complete. We cannot, however, be responsible for human error, typographical mistakes, or variations in individual work.